Tips for Reading Together

Children learn best when reading is fun.

- Talk about the title and the pictures on the cover.

- Discuss what you think the story might be about.

- Read the story together, inviting your child to read as much of it as they can.

- Give lots of praise as your child reads, and help them when necessary.

- Try different ways of helping if they get stuck on a word. For example, get them to say the first sound of the word, or break it into chunks, or read the whole sentence again, trying to guess the word. Focus on the meaning.

- Re-read the story later, encouraging your child to read as much of it as they can.

Children enjoy re-reading stories and this helps to build their confidence.

Have fun!

Dad's Grand Plan

Written by Roderick Hunt

Illustrated by Alex Brychta

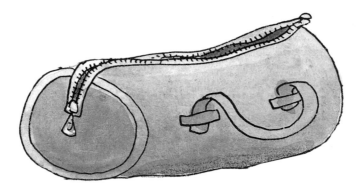

OXFORD

UNIVERSITY PRESS

Read these words before you begin the story:

laughed

crossly

washing

wrong

chimney

drove

middle

caught

soot

should

thirsty

fallen

stopped

Find words that end in *ed* like *wanted*.

Everyone was excited. It was holiday
time. Kipper couldn't wait.

"Only two days to go!" he said.

Chip looked at Floppy. He was running
round and round. They all laughed at him.
"See! Even Floppy is excited," said Chip.

Mum came in. She gave a big sigh.
"Dad wants a family meeting," she said.
"What's that?" asked Kipper.

"Dad has a Grand Plan."

"A Grand Plan?" said Chip. "What's a Grand Plan?"

"I don't like the sound of it," said Biff.

Everyone sat at the table. Dad had made a long list of jobs.

"I want everyone to help, then nobody gets cross," he said.

Everyone looked at the list. They all
had jobs to do. Mum liked Dad's Grand
Plan. Chip was not so sure!

"I've packed my bag," said Biff.

"And I've packed *my* bag," said Kipper.

"I have not packed yet," said Dad.

"Why not?" asked Mum.

"I can't find my socks," said Dad, crossly.

The socks were in the washing machine.

"Why were they in there?" asked Dad.

"That was where you put them," said Mum.

It was time to go. Dad's Grand Plan
had worked. Nothing had gone wrong.
"There's still time," whispered Chip.

Mum drove the car. Kipper was fed up.
He didn't want to sit in the middle.
"You can take turns," said Mum.

Kipper was hot. He began to moan.

"Can we stop for a drink?" said Chip.

"No," said Dad. "It will make us late."

Kipper wanted to change seats, but
Dad didn't want to stop.

"Maybe we should," said Mum.

"Yes, we are all thirsty," said Biff.

Mum saw a place and stopped. She
looked in the back of the car.

"Where's Floppy?" gasped Mum.
"We can't have forgotten him!"

But it was true. They had forgotten
Floppy.

"We'll have to go back for him,"
said Mum.

"So much for Dad's Grand Plan,"
said Biff.

They went back and got Floppy. But
now they were late. Mum drove fast.

"Slow down, Mum," said Kipper. "I
feel sick."

There was a bump.

"What was that?" asked Dad.

A bag had fallen off the roof rack.

Mum stopped the car.

The bag was in the road. It had come open. There were clothes everywhere.

"They look like Dad's clothes," said Biff.

Dad's socks were in the road. His
shirts were in the hedge. His pants were
in a tree. The children couldn't help
laughing.

"Don't stand there laughing," said
Dad. "Help me pick up my clothes."
"This wasn't in Dad's Grand Plan,"
said Mum.

At last they got to the holiday cottage. Next to it was a little stream. There was a rope swing on the tree.

"It looks great!" said Kipper.

Dad unlocked the door. Everyone
went inside.

"There's soot everywhere!" said Dad.
"It has come from the chimney."

"What's that?" said Mum.

A black bird was in the room.

"It's a crow!" said Dad.

"It came down the chimney," said Mum.

Dad caught the crow and let it out.
Everyone was sorry for it.

"I'm glad it's gone," said Biff. "But
what a mess it's made!"

"Cleaning up soot wasn't in Dad's Grand Plan," said Biff.

"Nor was having my pants in a tree!" laughed Dad.

Think about the story

Word Search

d	h	z	r	j	u	m	p	d	y
i	s	h	i	r	t	s	q	e	c
b	a	e	s	h	o	h	a	t	v
f	y	d	o	i	f	o	s	w	h
a	f	u	k	r	l	r	v	b	a
f	x	l	j	f	y	t	e	p	p
k	h	s	o	c	k	s	g	a	x
z	m	l	r	p	a	n	k	n	k
i	k	j	u	m	p	e	r	t	r
o	e	n	a	x	l	y	p	s	u

Find these items in the word search:

socks   pants   jumper   hat
shorts   shirts   floppy

Useful common words repeated in this story and other books in the series:

everyone excited couldn't laughed what's nobody
middle moan stopped gasped everywhere holiday
Names in the story: Dad Floppy Mum Biff Chip Kipper

More books for you to enjoy

Level 1: Getting Ready

- The Snowman
- Funny Fish
- Picnic Time
- Silly Races
- Dad's Birthday
- Mum's New Hat

Level 2: Starting to Read

- Poor Old Rabbit!
- Super Dad
- The Monster Hunt
- I Can Trick a Tiger
- Floppy and the Bone
- Ouch!

Level 3: Becoming a Reader

- Missing!
- The Old Tree Stump
- The Raft Race
- The Real Floppy
- Dragon Danger
- The Spaceship

Level 4: Building Confidence

- Arctic Adventure
- Looking After Gran
- Hungry Floppy
- Shrinking Powder
- Husky Adventure
- Trapped!

Level 5: Reading with Confidence

- The Hairy-Scary Monster
- The Golden Touch
- The Lost Voice
- The Palace Statues
- The Secret of the Sands
- Mountain Rescue

OXFORD
UNIVERSITY PRESS

Great Clarendon Street,
Oxford OX2 6DP

Text © Roderick Hunt 2002
Illustrations © Alex Brychta 2002
First published 2002

This edition published 2110

Read at Home Series Editors:
Kate Ruttle, Annemarie Young

British Library Cataloguing
in Publication Data available

ISBN: 9780198387756

10 9 8 7 6 5 4 3 2 1

Printed in China by Imago

Have more fun with Read at Home

- Floppy's Activity Book — Kate Ruttle • Alex Brychta
- First Dictionary
- Rhyming Games
- At the Dentist — Roderick Hunt • Alex Brychta
- Helping Your Child to Read